Table of Contents

Introduction

After ten years of global conflict with al Qaeda and other like-minded groups, the time has come to reassess the threat which al Qaeda represents and determine the parameters within which it operates.[1] Questions regarding its continued validity as a threat, its capability to employ synchronized tactical actions, and its ability to act as a learning organization all must be addressed in order to better understand this enemy of the United Sates, as well as to better prepare and defend against it.

Al Qaeda's early experiences fighting the Soviet occupation in Afghanistan left a profound impact on the organization in its ability to develop an overarching strategy. These formative experiences greatly aided the fledgling organization to become a preeminent transnational power. While al Qaeda had success against the Soviets, it knew that the next battle with a conventional military force could end tragically. Therefore, as al Qaeda grew, its doctrine and organization evolved. Taking the lesson it learned in its fight with the Soviets, it shifted tactics to terrorism and suicide attacks as its weapon of choice when battling Western powers. While its tactics have changed, the strategic goal of al Qaeda has been consistent.

Research Question

The research question this monograph will attempt to answer is: Does al Qaeda practice operational art? Borrowing from United States Army doctrine, this monograph will define operational art as the pursuit of strategic objectives, in whole or in part, through the arrangement of tactical actions in time, space, and purpose.[2]

---

[1] Al Qaeda; Arabic: القاعدة "The Base" alternatively spelled al Qaida or al Qa'ida are all one in the same for the remainder of this monograph

[2] Department of the Army, *Army Doctrinal Publication 3-0 Unified Land Operations* (Washington, DC: Government Printing Office, 2011), 9. Hereafter cited as *ADP 3-0* 2011. US Army doctrine was used versus Joint Doctrine as al Qaeda primarily operates as a land force, in some ways closely resembling special forces teams conducting highly targeted operations.

Hypothesis

Prior to reviewing the complete data set, it is believed that al Qaeda does indeed practice operational art. While al Qaeda has been inconsistent with many aspects of its operations, one of the most consistent threads of al Qaeda operations has been the overarching goals of the organization. This consistent strategic pursuit will be apparent in the selection of its targets through the information operations campaigns it has embarked on. Al Qaeda has not achieved its strategic goals, and is considered by many experts to be close to defeat. However, operational art is not a panacea for victory. Well-defined strategic objectives do not necessarily guarantee victory and the critics of this hypothesis and subsequent findings must bear that in mind. The consistency of the strategic goals also assist in the evaluation of operational art, as the stability of the end point assists in the endeavor to determine if tactical actions are being synchronized to steer towards that goal.

Method

To adequately test the hypothesis it is imperative that the strategic goals be defined. Once those are defined, this monograph will select two case studies that involve tactical action(s) by al Qaeda to test three results of those actions against the strategic goals of the organization. In some cases, it is believed that the actions will result in the attainment of strategic goals, while in others, the goal will not be realized and in fact the opposite effect may occur. The success or failure of a tactical action is not the focus of this study, and it is imperative that the reader not discount the existence of operational level planning and operational art even if the tactical attack is thwarted. The intent behind the timing, placement, and aim of the tactical actions and their linkage to other similar actions are more important to the assessment of whether operational art exists in al Qaeda's operations. These case studies will be distilled using three elements of operational art: center of gravity, lines of operations, and operational reach.

The Base

> [T]his matter isn't about any specific person and...is not about the al-Qai`dah Organization. We are the children of an Islamic Nation, with Prophet Muhammad as its leader, our Lord is one...and all the true believers are brothers. So the situation isn't like the West portrays it, that there is an "organization" with a specific name and so on. That particular name is very old. It was born without any intention from us. Brother Abu Ubaida... created a military base to train the young men to fight against the vicious, arrogant, brutal, terrorizing Soviet empire... So this place was called The Base, as in a training base, so this name grew and became. We aren't separated from this nation. We are the children of a nation, and we are an inseparable part of it, and from those public demonstrations which spread from the far east, from the Philippines, to Indonesia, to Malaysia, to India, to Pakistan, reaching Mauritania... and so we discuss the conscience of this nation.[3]

Al Qaeda serves as an informal organizational structure for extremist Arab-Afghans, along with thousands of recruits and supporters in some 55 countries. The al Qaeda network has been linked to various terrorist operations, such as the 1993 World Trade Center Bombing in New York, the 1996 bombing of Khobar Towers in Saudi Arabia, the 1998 United States Embassy bombings in East Africa, the 2000 attack of the destroyer USS Cole in Aden, Yemen, and the 2001 destruction of the World Trade Center in New York.[4]

The history of al Qaeda is a journey through conflict and turmoil. The organization emerged from the Mekhtab-al-Khidemat (MAK), the Afghan mujahedeen services office, around 1989. Osama bin Laden was the central figure of the organization known as al Qaeda prior to his death in May 2011.[5] His influence to the creation of this transnational organization began early in his life. Born in 1957 in Saudi Arabia, he was the seventeenth of 51 children of Muhammad bin

---

[3] Osama bin Laden, "Transcript of Bin Laden's October Interview," Cable News Network, http://articles.cnn.com/2002-02-05/world/binladen.transcript_1_incitement-fatwas-al-qaeda-organization?_s=PM:asiapcf (accessed Apr 01, 2012).

[4] Yonah Alexander and Michael S. Swetnam, *Usama Bin Laden's Al Qaida: Profile of a Terrorist Network* (New York: Transnational Publishers, 2001), 1.

[5] Jeffery B. Cozzens, "Approaching Al-Qaeda's Warfare: Function, Culture, and Grand Strategy," in *Mapping Terrorism Research,* ed. Magnus Ranstorp (New York: Routledge, 2007), 129.

Laden. His father was of Yemeni descent and his mother a Saudi. Muhammad founded the Bin Laden construction group in 1931, which was responsible for the building of holy mosques, highways, and palaces throughout Saudi Arabia. During this time, the company amassed a fortune worth billions of dollars.[6] Relationships built between prominent members of Saudi Royalty and bin Laden's family established a foundation of influential people in bin Laden's life. With the pursuit of a civil-engineering degree from King Abdul-Aziz University in Jeddah, Saudi Arabia, Osama bin Laden was being groomed to assume his role in the family business until the life altering events of the Siege on Mecca and the Soviet Union's occupation of Afghanistan occurred.[7]

These events, occurring around the time of his college graduation in 1980, inspired bin Laden to rally for Mujahedeen fighters to participate in the struggle against the communist grip over Afghanistan. By 1984, Osama bin Laden had provided machinery, money, and fighters to MAK, the Afghan mujahedeen services office, and built the first "guesthouse" in Peshawar, Pakistan, which would become the first station for recruits.[8] By 1986, his personal success as a military commander compelled him to create a separate branch of the MAK, and by 1989 he completed his efforts to separate from the MAK. Bin Laden needed a method of keeping track of fighters and fellow supporters, which sparked the concept of al Qaeda.[9] Although al Qaeda's headquarters remained in Pakistan, bin Laden moved back to Saudi Arabia to tout the recent victories in Afghanistan and warn of upcoming Iraqi aggression against Kuwait. His speeches

---

[6] Lawrence J. Bevy, ed., *Al-Qaeda: An Organization To Be Reckoned With* (New York: Novinka, 2004), 4.

[7] Yaroslav Trofimov, *The Siege of Mecca* (New York: Doubleday, 2007), 225.

[8] Jane Corbin, *Al Qaeda: In Search of the Terror Network that Threatens the World* (New York: Nation Books, 2002), 38.

[9] Ibid., 40.

further detailed failures of the Saudi Government, which led them to ban bin Laden from leaving the country.[10]

After the Iraqi invasion of Kuwait, bin Laden was distraught that the Saudi government had sought and received western governments' help. He immediately moved back to Pakistan to continue the war against the communist puppet government of Afghanistan and attempted to mediate a treaty in the Afghan civil war. His failed efforts forced him to seek a new location in order to establish his organization. Soon after, an opportunity arose in Sudan. The strict Islamist ideology of the new regime under the National Islamic Front appealed to him, and the regime sought out bin Laden's help. Additionally, the vast amounts of construction opportunities presented a support system for the expansion of the al Qaeda organization.[11] Sudan became the new face of al Qaeda. It was a perfect fit for the new network. Sudan was characterized by coercion and corruption and welcoming to foreign Arab fighters that had no sanctuary in their home nations. Through 1996, bin Laden built his organization and experimented with terrorist operations in Yemen, Saudi Arabia, Somalia, and New York, among other locations. The Sudanese government, finally feeling international pressure for hosting bin Laden, requested he leave the country. No longer a citizen of Saudi Arabia and with his assets frozen, he moved back to Afghanistan to reestablish a stronghold for al Qaeda and to find a new location to build his organization.[12]

Bin Laden's experience with MAK was significant for three reasons. First, he learned how to finance, man, equip, and organize an army.[13] Second, he learned how to employ tactics

---

[10] Bruce Riedel, *The Search For Al Qaeda* (Washington DC: Brookings Institution Press, 2008), 41.

[11] Ibid., 44.

[12] John Rollins, "Al Qaeda and Affiliates: Historical Perspective, Global Presence, and Implications for U.S. Policy," in *Al Qaeda: Background, Evolution, and Assessment*, ed. Alice F. Esposito (New York: Nova Science Publishers, Inc., 2010), 6.

[13] Reidel, *The Search for Al-Qaeda*, 46.

across space and time to meet strategic goals. Finally, and most importantly, bin Laden believed

he had developed a strategy to defeat a super power and began altering his organization's

doctrine. Despite Soviets superior material power, they were seen by bin Laden as lacking faith; a

paper tiger, which ultimately could be defeated, in time, by a much smaller and very determined

force.[14] Bin Laden now shifted his focus to the United States.

Al Qaeda's Strategy

> O American people, I am speaking to tell you about the ideal way to
> avoid another Manhattan, about war and its causes and results. Security is an
> important foundation of human life and free people do not squander their
> security… It is known that those who hate freedom do not possess proud souls
> like those of the 19, may God rest their souls. We fought you because we are free
> and because we want freedom for our nation. When you squander our security we
> squander yours.[15]

Policy and strategy are a useful starting point for understanding bin Laden's application

of operational art. The United States publishes its National Security and National Military

Strategies to unify efforts and resources to achieve the nation's interests. A similar perspective

that comes from the British National Security Strategy and more clearly explains the goals of

strategy states that "a combination of ends (what we are seeking to achieve), ways (the ways by

which we seek to achieve those ends) and means (the resources we can devote to achieving the

ends)" must be arranged to best achieve objectives and balanced to prevent adversaries from

achieving theirs."[16] Al Qaeda, a transnational organization, is not a state but it does have policy

---

[14] Rollins, "Al Qaeda and Affiliates," 7. See also Yossef Bodansky, *Bin Laden: The Man Who Declared War on America* (New York: Random House, Inc., 1999), 56-65.

[15] Osama Bin Laden, "God knows it did not cross our minds to attack the towers," The Guardian, http://www.guardian.co.uk/world/2004/oct/30/alqaida.september11 (accessed Apr 1, 2012).

[16] David Cameron, "A Strong Britain in an Age of Uncertainty: The National Security Strategy 2010," http://www.official-documents.gov.uk/ (accessed Apr 1, 2012), 10. Hereafter cited as UK NSS 2010.

objectives and strategic goals that are much broader than the limited, local focus typical to terrorist organizations.

Al Qaeda's policy was to compel the United States to remove its troops from Saudi Arabia, and ultimately compel the United States to abandon its economic and military policies against Iraq, undermine the security relationship between the United States and Israel, and to dismantle the relationships between the United States and various Arab regimes.[17]

In his statements, bin Laden did not find issues with the decadence of Western culture, that mainstream arguments that emphasize Islam's rejection of drug and alcohol abuse, sexual permissiveness, illegitimacy, equality for women, and the west's tolerance of homosexuals, and secularism as motivating al Qaeda's actions.[18] Rather, bin Laden continually focused on the four policy objectives listed above. Bin Laden has consistently addressed these strategic objectives. To achieve his policy objectives, bin Laden had to compel the United States to abandon or alter its policy objectives. In order to meet these strategic goals raised the cost of the political object beyond its value to the United States. Bin Laden's rational calculus led him to believe that the end state and objectives are more valuable to him than to the United States and the West.[19]

The Crucible is Formed, Operationalizing the Strategy

With the defeat of the Soviets in Afghanistan and the subsequent fall of the Soviet Union, bin Laden believed Islam was facing only two remaining threats. In the past, most Islamic fundamentalist believed the critical battle was against the enemy who is near. They focused on

---

[17] Rohan Gunaratna, "Who is Al Qaeda?," *Jane's Intelligence Review*, Vol. 13, no. 8, (August 2001) http://www.mwarrior.com/alqaeda.htm (accessed Jan 23, 2012).

[18] Osama bin Laden, "Terrorism Against America Deserves To Be Praised," The Outlook Group, http://www.outlookindia.com/article.aspx?214141 (accessed Jan 23, 2012).

[19] Osama bin Laden, "Bin Laden's Warning," British Broadcasting Corporation, http://newsvote.bbc.co.uk/2/hi/south_asia/1585636.stm (accessed Jan 30, 2012).

the Arab defectors and were unsuccessful.[20] Uniquely, and perhaps wisely, bin Laden chose to set

his sights on the enemy who is afar first, and deal with Islamic defectors later. The enemy who is

afar was considered the West and its artificial creation, Israel, known by Islamic fundamentalists

as the Zionist entity. Al Qaeda would not separate these influences.[21] Specifically, bin Laden had

articulated the following operational objectives in support of his campaign strategy: 1) removal of

U.S. forces from the Arabian Peninsula and complete elimination of the American presence in the

Middle East, 2) return of Palestine to the Islamic community, and 3) to seek other means of

military power such as weapons of mass destruction to aid his effort.[22]

These operational objectives were not intended for al Qaeda agents exclusively, but for

Islamists worldwide, who bin Laden attempted to incorporate. The Islamic community was being

threatened, and bin Laden called for a defensive jihad. Unlike an offensive jihad, which Islam

requires only soldiers to fight, a defensive jihad is every Muslim's personal duty as bin Laden

stated, "To kill Americans and their allies, both civil and military, is an individual duty of every

Muslim who is able, in any country where this is possible."[23]

By developing his strategy and operationalizing it, he attempted to unite and gain support

from the Muslim community against a common outside enemy. He did not intend to defeat

America in a war, but rather intended to use the United States as a tool in order to promote the

realization of his strategic objectives. The emerging U.S. policy, in which President Bush stated,

that nations are either with the free world or the terrorists, helped bin Laden polarize the world as

---

[20] Hashim, S. Ahmed, "The Strategy of Usama Bin Laden and Al Qaeda," *Newport Papers,* ed. Andrew L. Ross (Newport: Naval War College, 2002): 20.

[21] Alexander and Swetnam, *Usama*, 43.

[22] Bernard Lewis, "License to Kill: Usama Bin Laden's Declaration of Jihad," *Foreign Affairs,* (November 1998), http://www.foreignaffairs.com/articles/54594/bernard-lewis/license-to-kill-usama-bin-ladins-declaration-of-jihad (accessed Mar 14, 2012).

[23] Ibid.

either true believers or infidels.[24] Bin Laden's strategy cast the United States as the villain, that after being provoked would retaliate militarily for al Qaeda's terrorist attacks, inflicting damage and causing the death of innocent Muslims throughout the world. The Islamic community's response, he believed, would be outrage and revolution, causing separation between state and society in the Middle East. The corrupt illegitimate governments allied with the West would find themselves adrift or be destroyed.[25] These are the conditions bin Laden sought to shape to execute his operational plan.

The Tactical Linkage

> Terrorising[sic] you, while you are carrying arms on our land, is a legitimate and morally demanded duty. . . . It is a duty now on every tribe in the Arab Peninsula to fight, Jihad, in the cause of Allah and to cleanse the land from those occupiers. . . . These youths know that: if one is not to be killed one will die (anyway) and the most honourable death is to be killed in the way of Allah.[26]

During the ten-year struggle with the Soviet Union, members of the future organization, al Qaeda, learned a great deal about implementing small decisive operations linked over time to achieve victory. In several memoirs discussing the attacks against the Soviet Union in Afghanistan, a dialogue of best practices and discovery learning dominated the thoughts of rising leaders, such as bin Laden.[27] The allure of endured combat fell out of favor with these young fighters after they experienced the lethality of Soviet's combined arms warfare. A change in tactics arose as the operational approach of al Qaeda evolved.

---

[24] Riedel, *The Search*, 51.

[25] Michael Scott Doran, "Somebody Else's Civil War," in *How Did This Happen? Terrorism and the New War*, ed. James F. Hoge, Jr. and Gideon Rose (New York: Public Affairs, 2001), 32.

[26] Osama bin Laden, "Declaration of War Against the Americans Occupying the Land of the Two Holy Places," http://www.pbs.org/newshour/terrorism/international/ fatwa_1996.html (accessed Apr 1, 2012).

[27] Abdul Salam Zaeef, *My Life With the Taliban* (New York: C Hurst & Co., 2010), 48.

The tactical building blocks that al Qaeda utilized to implement operations included assassination, bombing, chemical attacks, hijacking, hostage taking, kidnapping, sabotage, suicide and vehicular bombing. These tactics were rehearsed, practiced and codified as actions linked together in comprising operational plans to pursue strategic objectives.[28] The *Al Qaeda Handbook*, purportedly written by bin Laden, detailed the specifics of which tactics were best for employing bombs in multiple types of environments, techniques in creating mass casualties in densely populated areas, and basic information operations to quickly transmit messages to the global community.[29]

Assassination training had been provided to al Qaeda members using foreign fighters and training videos. Recovered film footage showed trainees studying a map of a western-style traffic intersection, and then carrying out an apparent military-style assassination attack on a motorcade. Other assassination styles shown in training videos included drive-by shootings and the use of grenades. This assassination tactic has not been widely used during al Qaeda's larger operations, but in cases such as the killing of Northern Alliance leader, Ahmed Shah Massoud, the method was quite successful.[30]

One of the most utilized tactics was the employment of improvised explosive devices or military munitions to cause a mass casualty incident or destroy a specific facility. The al Qaeda forces were trained to build these devices with remote triggers, sensors or timers. In the multiple chapters that describe destruction by blasting, bin Laden's book explains that "[e]xplosives are believed to be the safest weapon for the Mujahideen. [Using bombs] allows them to get away from enemy personnel and to avoid being arrested. An assassination using explosives doesn't

---

[28] Osama bin Laden, "The Al Qaeda Handbook," United States Department of Justice, http://www.justice.gov/ag/manualpart1_1.pdf (accessed Mar 14, 2012).

[29] Ibid. 13

[30] Alexander and Swetnam, *Usama*, 28.

leave any evidence or traces at the operation site. In addition, explosives strike the enemy with sheer terror and fright."[31]

Another tactic trained and codified is the use of a chemical agent against a population center, large gathering or areas with a high concentration of people, such as subway systems.[32] As described in their tactics manual, chemical attacks may make use of industrial chemicals that are readily accessible. These chemicals can be obtained through theft or hijacking of vehicles transporting them around the country. In a communication by al Qaeda spokesman Suleiman abu Ghaith he explained, "we have the right to kill four million Americans - two million of them children - and to exile twice as many and injure and cripple hundreds of thousands. We have the right to fight them by chemical and biological weapons, so they catch the fatal and unusual diseases that Muslims have caught due to their [United States] chemical and biological weapons."[33]

Another tactic used is the hijacking or forceful taking over of a plane, cruise ship or other large craft. The objective could be to obtain hostages in a mobile environment or as in the case on September 11, 2001, utilize the craft as a projectile in a suicide operation. In the event of the suicide mode of attack, private jets or chartered aircraft may also be used. Explosives would likely be utilized to offset the lower fuel load capability of the smaller aircraft.[34]

Yet another tactic is the hostage taking of an individual or group of people by one or more terrorists. The event may occur as part of a hijacking or at any gathering of people which provides a suitable environment for the al Qaeda forces. Hostages may be taken as part of an attempt to have specific demands met or simply as a manner of attracting maximum media

---

[31] Bin Laden, "Al Qaeda Handbook," 10.

[32] Ibid., 22.

[33] National Infrastructure Protection Center, "Terrorist Interest in Water Supply and SCADA Systems, Information Bulletin 02-001," National Water System, http://www.mrws.org/Terror/Bulletin.html (accessed Mar 14, 2012).

[34] Bin Laden, "Al Qaeda Handbook," 23.

coverage before killing the hostages by detonating an explosive device or through other means. Al Qaeda's training manual detailed the guidelines for beating and killing hostages. It goes on to say, "permission is granted to strike the nonbeliever who has no covenant until he reveals the news, information, and secrets of his people."[35]

Al Qaeda's abduction tactic proved significantly effective throughout its existence, particularly in the case of Daniel Pearl.[36] Al Qaeda acknowledges that this tactic requires a significant support infrastructure and encourages detailed planning prior to execution. Al Qaeda's training manual explains the detrimental cost to keep an abducted individual. The book sights religious leaders as endorsing such actions under a set of rules that must be closely followed.[37]

Sabotage remained a key element to al Qaeda's training curriculum. The organization defined sabotage as the tampering or destruction of critical components of transportation systems, power plants or other systems, which would result in a mass casualty incident, or severe disruption of services.[38] Sabotage may be carried out through physical or cyber means. According to FBI Information Bulletin 02-001: "United States law enforcement and intelligence agencies have received indications that al Qaeda members have sought information on Supervisory Control and Data Acquisition systems available on multiple web sites. [Al Qaeda] specifically sought information on water supply and wastewater management practices in the U.S. and abroad. There has also been interest in insecticides and pest control products at several web sites."[39]

The final and most utilized tactic is the suicide or vehicular bombing. These types of attacks are designed to inflict as many casualties as possible. Suicide bombers may combine both

---

[35] Bin Laden, "Al Qaeda Handbook," 28.

[36] Bernard-Henri Levy, *Who Killed Daniel Pearl?* (New York: Melville House Publishing, 2003), 112.

[37] Bin Laden, "Al Qaeda Handbook," 8.

[38] Ibid., 31.

[39] Ibid., 29.

suicide and vehicular bombings as in the 1998 East Africa Embassy Bombings.[40] This tactic has

significant amount of religious overtones to justify these actions. The goal, as the training manual

describes, focuses on the implementation of this sort of attack on public locations, transportation

systems, and ideological symbols to increase effectiveness.[41] This technique is preferred mainly

because it is seen by al Qaeda as attacking one of the centers of gravity of the weak western

powers, their unwillingness to sustain casualties.

This monograph analyzes historical examples of al Qaeda operations, the tactics

discussed above will serve as doctrinal techniques utilized by the organization's forces. In the

strategic framework outlined in the United Kingdom National Security Strategy, these techniques

represent the methods of attack, or ways, that Al Qaeda will implement to build the campaigns or

operations it believes will achieve its strategic goals.[42] Understanding why, and in which manner

al Qaeda fights lays the foundational framework needed to understand the ends it seeks, and the

ways and means it will use to get there. Now it is possible to examine their tactical actions and

determine if there is an intentional effort to organize these actions as required by operational art.

Linking the Strategic to the Tactical

Operational art as a codified theory is a recent addition to military thought. As recently as

2011, the United States Army has redefined the term as "the pursuit of strategic objectives, in

whole or in part, through the arrangement of tactical actions in time, space, and purpose."[43] The

foundation of operational art develops from the early twentieth century works of Russian and

Soviet military experiences. G.S. Isserson in *The Evolution of Operational Art* analyzed past wars

to establish a framework to evaluate campaigns and metrics the applicability of operational art in

---

[40] National Infrastructure Protection Center, "Information Bulletin 02-001."

[41] Bin Laden, "Al Qaeda Handbook," 5.

[42] UK NSS 2010, 10.

[43] *ADP 3-0* 2011, 9.

emerging Russian doctrine.[44] His theories sought to overcome the positional deadlock encountered in World War I with the employment of large motorized and tank formations, front offensive and defensive operations, breakthrough of the enemy's defensive position under various circumstances of the situation, and exploitation of success in an offensive operation. His theory, deep operations, became the first significant contribution to the development of operational art.

Arguably, the most significant work done in operational art development is Jacob W. Kipp. Kipp's thorough analysis of the Soviet development of operational art further built upon the outcome of Isserson and his colleagues' establishment of the new theory.[45] Another contemporary historian, James J. Schneider, provides a prescriptive approach in identifying operational art during the American Civil War in *Vulcan's Anvil: The American Civil War*.[46] Dr. Schneider's work explored the connections between the crisis of the command and control of mass armies and the impact of mass industrialization, of fire and maneuver on the conduct of campaigns.

The work of Shimon Naveh provides an overview of the development of operational art theory from Soviet deep operations theory to American air land battle doctrine. Mr. Naveh's work emphasized a systems or design approach to executing operations. He highlighted Soviet operational art as a special case because it combined a systems approach with an emphasis upon shock and disruption in the conduct of deep operations. Naveh noted that the Soviets context to deep operations was specific to their context and universally applicable.[47] The need for liberation from operational art in this context was the result of an adaptive opponent who no longer

---

[44] Georgii Samoilovich Isserson, *The Evolution of Operational Art*, trans. Bruce W. Menning (Moscow: The State Military Publishing House of the USSR People's Defense, 1937), 22.

[45] Jacob W. Kipp, "The Origins of Soviet Operational Art 1917-1936," in *The Historical Perspectives of the Operational Art*, ed. Michael Detlef Krause and R. Cody Phillips (Washington, DC: GPO, 2005), 215.

[46] James J. Schneider, *Vulcan's Anvil: The American Civil War and the Foundation of Operational Art Theoretical Paper No. Four* (Fort Leavenworth: United States Army Command and General Staff College, 2004), 30.

[47] Shimon Naveh, *In Pursuit of Military Excellence: The Evolution of Operational Theory* (London: Frank Cass, 1997), 209-238.

practiced mass industrial war but had adopted the instruments of insurgency and terrorism to conflict in the 21st century. All of these works contributed important elements to the ideas behind the United States Army's current thoughts on operational art.

Operational art must be addressed to establish the framework for investigating al Qaeda's operations. Underlying these definitions is the nature of policy and its interdependency with war. Military theorist Carl von Clausewitz describes war as an extension of politics by other means.[48] This statement is significant because it bounds military action to policy. The aims of policy should always seek continuous advantage because interaction will always occur between the opposing nations in some form.[49] Thus, the political authorities define the type of war the military will fight and impose restrictions to prevent military action from producing harmful political effects.[50] Additionally, military action will inherently create unforeseen strategic challenges and reveal new information which may lead to the refinement of strategy and policy. Therefore, political authorities must be closely integrated with military planners to ensure military action both supports and informs policy.

Larger and more intense wars in the 19th and 20th centuries prevented political authorities from focusing solely on the conduct of military operations due to the critical importance of the evolving homeland functions required to sustain and prosecute wars. The role of the commander changed to include both political and strategic discourse to enable a common understanding of what is to be achieved politically and what can be achieved tactically.[51] The campaign command thus came to serve three primary functions. First, it provided the tactical

---

[48] Michael Howard and Peter Paret, *Carl von Clausewitz, On War*, 1st Edition (Princeton: Princeton University Press, 1989), 87.

[49] Everett Dolman, *Pure Strategy: Power and Policy in the Space and Information Age* (New York: 2005), 14-15.

[50] Albert C. Pierce, "War: Strategy vs. Ethics, Ethics and Strategy?" (PhD diss., University California, Berkley, 2002), 4-6.

[51] Teun Van Dijk and Walter Kintsch, *Strategies of Discourse Comprehension* (Waltham, Massachusetts: Academic Press, 1983), 224.

perspective to the development of strategy. Second, it unified a wide range of military options under one common purpose to ensure that tactical actions were purposeful in achieving the ends of policy and strategy. Finally, it integrated and assisted in the sustainment of the wide array of forces participating in the campaign.[52]

The purpose of the campaign is to achieve the strategic aim. With the complexities and uncertainties that exist in any long-term human endeavor, a strategic aim must be conceptually based because what is possible to achieve is heavily influenced by the effects of the actions taken along the way.[53] The effects of these actions simply cannot be predicted with any precision at the beginning of the conflict because of the unlimited interdependent variables in the environment. Therefore, the campaign commander generates a broad, long-range plan, or operational approach, to guide decision-making and selection of short-term objectives to progress towards the strategic aim.[54] The United States Army doctrine characterizes operational art into eleven elements.[55] Although there is no need for all eleven elements to be present in a campaign for operational art to be present, a series of tactical actions that failed to embody any of the eleven elements would likely not meet the test for operational art. In such instances it would not be unusual for the military violence to either fail to meet the strategic objectives, or indeed at times to act contrary to the achievement of those objectives.

Analysis of Two Campaigns

The case studies will review two campaigns which al Qaeda has participated. The first will be the campaign against the United States that will begin with the first attack on the World

---

[52] U.S. Department of the Army, *FM 3-0 Operations* (Washington, DC: GPO, 2008), 6-2. Hereafter cited as *FM 3-0*.

[53] U.S. Department of the Army, *FM 6-22 Army Leadership* (Washington, DC: GPO, 2006), 2-3.

[54] Ibid., 2-4.

[55] *FM 3-0*, 7-4.

Trade Center in New York in 1993. This case study will examine the operations al Qaeda executed exclusively against American targets, the strategic aim the operations were designed to move towards, and then assess whether or not there was evidence of operational art. The second case analyzed is the campaign that al Qaeda undertook in 2004 to discourage allies of the United States from participation in the invasion and occupation of Iraq. This case study will explore the actions that al Qaeda executed in Spain and England in 2004 and 2005. Both case studies will use three elements of operational art: lines of effort, center of gravity analysis, and operational reach, to determine if al Qaeda employed these elements of operational art to improve its ability to meet the strategic objective. The case studies will also explore if the tactical action served no apparent linkage of strategic purpose, therefore qualifying as an act of senseless violence and falling out of the scope of this analysis. To support a thorough understanding of the argument, it is important to first define the elements that are to be analyzed.

The first element, center of gravity is defined as the source of power that provides moral or physical strength, freedom of action, or will to act.[56] This definition states in modern terms the classic description offered by Clausewitz: "the hub of all power and movement, on which everything depends."[57] The center of gravity is a vital analytical tool for planning operations. It provides a focal point, identifying sources of strength and weakness. Both cases will examine whether or not al Qaeda had identified a center of gravity, and if so further examine if the actions taken were intended to attack that center of gravity.

Center of gravity analysis is thorough and detailed. Faulty conclusions drawn from hasty or abbreviated analysis can adversely affect operations, waste critical resources, and incur undue risk.[58] Thoroughly understanding the operational environment helps commanders identify and

---

[56] *FM 3-0*, 7-2.

[57] Michael Howard and Peter Paret, *On War*, 583.

[58] *FM 3-0*, 7-4.

target enemy centers of gravity. This understanding encompasses how enemies organize, fight, and make decisions. It also includes their physical and moral strengths and weaknesses. In addition, commanders should understand how military forces interact with other government and civilian agencies as the center of gravity in a particular conflict need not be a military target.[59]

The next element of operational art that will assist in examining al Qaeda is lines of operations. A line of operations is a line that defines the directional orientation of a force in time and space in relation to the enemy and links the force with its base of operations and objectives.[60] Lines of operations connect a series of decisive points that lead to control of geographic or force-oriented objectives. Operations designed using lines of operations generally consist of a series of actions executed according to a well-defined sequence. Commanders synchronize activities along complementary lines of operations to achieve the end state. Lines of operations portray the more traditional links between objectives, decisive points, and centers of gravity.[61] In the case studies addressed identifying whether or not tactical actions were actually lines of operations will be essential to proving the hypothesis that al Qaeda practices operational art.

The final element of operational art used to study al Qaeda attacks is operational reach. Operational reach is the distance and duration across which a unit can successfully employ military capabilities.[62] Operational reach is described in United States Army doctrine as a tether, stretching and contracting to ensure the force is protected and can endure while awaiting battle and strong enough at the moment of battle.[63] The protection of the force, in reference to operational reach, discusses protecting the minimal requirements needed to execute and operation

---

[59] Ibid.

[60] Ibid., 7-6.

[61] Ibid. A decisive point is a geographic place, specific key event, critical factor, or function that, when acted upon, allows a commander to gain a marked advantage over an adversary or contributes materially to achieving success.

[62] Ibid., 7-12.

[63] Ibid., 7-13.

as well as the protection gained by extending operational reach. Endurance refers to the ability to employ combat power anywhere for long periods regardless of the distance from its source of power or the difficulty of the environment.[64] Finally, commanders anticipate how the enemy's actions might disrupt operations and then determine the strength and capabilities required to ensure success.[65] These three elements of operational reach, protection, endurance, and strength in battle, will assist in understanding how al Qaeda implemented operational art through time and space. In the case studies examined, demonstrating operational reach will assist in determining if al Qaeda practices operational art as efforts to create and extend operational reach are by their very nature intentional, and thus demonstrative of the mens rea needed to reach the definition of operational art.

Central to the argument of this monograph is accepting that al Qaeda integrates these three elements of operational art into its campaigns to achieve its strategic objectives. Although it may not possess a doctrinal manual that lays out the tenets and terms typical of formalized western militaries, the conceptual thought required to develop the campaign that integrate centers of gravity, lines of operations, and operational reach will suffice to prove operational art exists for this terrorist organization.

The American Campaign

The United States became the focal point of bin Laden's strategy in the aftermath of Iraq's aggression towards Kuwait in 1991. In his mind, Saudi Arabia betrayed its lineage to Islamic principles by inviting the United States to thwart the aggressive seizure of Kuwait by Iraq. The stage was set for the United States to use Saudi Arabia as a staging area for offensive operations and as a base for its continuing presence in the region into the indefinite future. This

---

[64] Ibid., 7-13.

[65] Ibid., 7-14.

resulted in the development of the first Campaign of al Qaeda: remove United States forces from the Arabian Peninsula and eliminate the American presence in the Middle East.

This case study examines five tactical operations focused on American objectives in four countries across the span of 8 years, all executed to facilitate the removal of the Unites States forces from the Middle East. The campaign begins in New York City on February 26, 1993 with the bombing of the North Tower of the World Trade Center. The following study will review the events of the Khobar Towers bombing in Saudi Arabia on June 25, 1998 and then the simultaneous bombings of the United States Embassies on August 7, 1998. The final linkages will explore the attack on the USS Cole on October 12, 2000 and the attacks in America on September 11, 2001.[66] These operations provide insight as to how al Qaeda learned, progressed, and innovated in its practice of operational art.

Attack in New York

The 1993 bombings of the World Trade Center occurred on February 26, 1993, when a truck bomb was detonated below the North Tower of the World Trade Center in New York City. The explosion was intended to knock the North Tower into the South Tower, bringing both towers down and killing thousands of people. It failed to do so, but it did kill six people and injured more than a thousand.[67] This first attempt by al Qaeda to bring down the towers provided a glimpse into the operational mindset of the leadership. Ramzi Yousef, the individual responsible for leading the attack, was trained in Afghanistan during the war with the Soviet Union.[68] Al Qaeda utilized its tactical experience gained during this war to begin the campaign of

---

[66] National Commission on Terrorist Attacks Upon the United States, *9-11 Commission Report* (Washington, DC: GPO, 2004), 18. Hereafter cited as 9-11 Report

[67] Doran, "Civil War," 33.

[68] Brian M. Jenkins, "The Organization Men: Anatomy of a Terrorist Attack," in *How Did This Happen? Terrorism and the New War*, ed. James F. Hoge, Jr. and Gideon Rose (New York: Public Affairs, 2001), 12.

removing the United States from the Middle East.[69] This operation provided a glimpse into al Qaeda's initial ability to exercise operational reach. The attack was not carried out by disaffected local Muslims loosely motivated by al Qaeda propaganda. Al Qaeda assisted directly in placing the individual with the right technology, expertise, and withdrawal plan to pursue success. The problem of building the right type of bomb for the infrastructure was not identified until after the attack failed, however it would be overcome in the next attack.

The 1993 World Trade Center bombing revealed indicators that this type of operation would become the norm in the future. Although the operation did not succeed, al Qaeda learned a valuable lesson in the wake of the event. The United States' response focused on the internal security to its physical infrastructure. The lack of response from the United States to prosecute al Qaeda created a sense of sanctuary for al Qaeda and reinforced their belief that the United States was weak and unwilling to suffer many casualties to defend its policy on the Arabian Peninsula. Additionally, al Qaeda's analysis of the center of gravity by attacking a civilian target will be further examined as other operations come to fruition. The argument that al Qaeda fully analyzed the United States' center of gravity as the will of the American people has yet come to the forefront.

Attack in Saudi Arabia

Following the attack on the Khobar Towers in Saudi Arabia, al Qaeda refined lessons learned in the previous operation and identified best practices that would be honed for future attacks. Meanwhile, in Saudi Arabia the United States military and members of the intelligence community utilized an 8-story building, the Khobar Towers, located near an affluent part of

---

[69] Vahid Brown, ed., *Cracks in the Foundation: Leadership Schisms in Al-Qaida 1989–2006* (West Point: Combating Terrorism Center Press, 2007), 7-11.

country, as temporary housing during military support operations in the region.[70] The security

around the building was not adequate as there was little to no offset between busy commercial

streets, the wall around the compound, and the buildings inside. Ultimately, the bombing killed

19 United States service members and injured hundreds more. In the view of al Qaeda, this

operation became the standard by which success would be measured.

The attackers prepared for the operation by hiding large amounts of explosive materials

and timing devices in paint cans and 50-kilogram bags underground in Qatif near Khobar. The

bomb was a mixture of gasoline and explosive powder placed in the tank of a sewage tanker

truck.[71] The delivery capabilities of al Qaeda's attacks were limited to devices that could carry

large amounts explosives. This technique becomes a limiting factor in future operations and

eventually required a shift in tactics. This shift, although significant, did not change the way al

Qaeda applied operational art.

Initially, the attackers attempted to enter the compound at the main checkpoint at around

9:43 p.m. local time. When they were denied access by U.S. military personnel, they drove a

Datsun scout vehicle, another car, and the bomb truck to a parking lot adjacent to the towers. A

chain link security fence and a line of small trees separated the parking lot, used for a local

mosque and park, from the housing compound. The perimeter of the towers were approximately

72 feet from the fence line, with a perimeter road between the fence and building which was often

used by military personnel for jogging. The first car entered the parking lot and signaled the

others by flashing headlights. The bomb truck and a getaway vehicle followed shortly after. The

men parked the truck next to the fence and left in the third vehicle. The bomb exploded three to

four minutes later at approximately 9:50 p.m. local time.[72]

---

[70] Perry D. Jamieson, *Khobar Towers: Tragedy and Response* (Washington, DC: GPO, 2008), 12.
[71] Ibid., 26.
[72] Ibid., 44-48.

Al Qaeda's ability to adjust its plan showed adaptability and ingenuity at the tactical level. The operational success resonated later when United States and Coalition military personnel at Khobar and Dhahran were subsequently relocated to Prince Sultan Air Base, a remote and highly secure Royal Saudi Air Force installation near Al-Kharj in central Saudi Arabia, approximately 70 miles from Riyadh.[73] United States, United Kingdom, and French military operations would continue at Prince Sultan until late 2003, when French forces withdrew and United States and UK operations shifted to Al Udeid Air Base in Qatar. This small victory of moving western troops away from the population center in Saudi Arabia was seen as a successful operation and laid the foundation for future attacks that would maximize operational reach. It also contributed to the developing thought that casualties were a center of gravity not just for the United States, but also for its western allies.

The operation in Saudi Arabia corrected the tactical problems that contributed to failure in New York. The physical type of target remained consistent to al Qaeda's approach of pursuing its strategic end state but the attack on military service members revealed a refocus the center of gravity. Although the result of removing the majority of US service members from the country of Saudi Arabia eventually occurred, the desired strategic aim of removing all American forces from the Middle East was yet to be achieved. The United States response was less focused on identifying an organization to hold responsible for the attack and more focused on the internal investigation of why the intelligence community had so many knowledge gaps that prevented any effective warning of the impending attack.[74] Again, al Qaeda capitalized on the lack of scrutiny to learn and develop new ways to apply varying tactics to pursue strategic goals.[75] In its first two attacks against the United States, al Qaeda demonstrated a developing line of operation that

---

[73] Ibid., 80.

[74] Ibid., 212.

[75] Bodansky, *Bin Laden*, 189-192.

incorporated tactical lessons learned into future attacks, increasing operational reach, and the beginnings of an idea on what al Qaeda thought the US center of gravity might be.

Attack in East Africa

An emboldened al Qaeda rose to the forefront of the international community with the simultaneous attacks on the US embassies in Tanzania and Kenya. This event marked the eighth anniversary of the arrival of United States troops in Saudi Arabia, which made the strategic message quite clear to the United States government, that al Qaeda wanted the United States out of the Middle East.[76] The complexity and success of its plan revealed an organization continuing to learn from its experiences and experimenting with new ways to employ and synchronize tactical actions. This third attack in the series of this campaign against America, presented a new element of operational art: lines of operations. Although the detonations occurred within ten minutes of one another, and may have represented the element of operational art of simultaneity as well, that is not a focus of this research.

On the morning of August 7, 1998, suicide bombers, in trucks loaded with explosives parked outside the embassies in Dar es Salaam, Tanzania and Nairobi, Kenya attacked within minutes of one another.[77] In Nairobi, approximately 212 people were killed, and an estimated 4,000 wounded; in Dar es Salaam, the attack killed at least 11 and wounded 85.[78] Although the attacks were directed at American facilities, the vast majority of casualties were local citizens with only 12 Americans killed.[79]

---

[76] James J. F. Forrest, *Countering Terrorism and Insurgency in the 21st Century* (Westport: Greenwood Publishing Group, 2007), 103.

[77] Ibid., 106.

[78] Ibid.

[79] Ibid., 112. See also Bodansky, *Bin Laden*, 249-257.

The explosion damaged the embassy building and flattened the adjacent Ufundi building where most victims were killed, mainly students and staff of a secretarial college housed there. The heat from the blast was channeled between the buildings towards an alleyway where a packed commuter bus was burned.[80] A large number of eye injuries occurred because people in buildings nearby who had heard the first explosion of the hand grenade and the shooting, went to their office windows to observe the turmoil when the main blast occurred and shattered the windows.[81]

Meanwhile, the atlas truck in Dar es Salaam was being driven by Hamdan Khalif Alal, a former al Qaeda camp trainer who had arrived in the country only a few days earlier.[82] This commitment of utilizing experienced members of al Qaeda demonstrated a use of operational reach. The death toll was less than in Nairobi as the U.S. embassy was located outside the city center on a large plot with no immediate buildings close to the gate where the explosion occurred.

Following the attacks, a group calling itself the "Liberation Army for Holy Sites" took credit for the bombings. It was later identified that Osama bin Laden participated heavily in the planning and financing of the operation. As the ties to al Qaeda became clear, the United States placed bin Laden on its most wanted list.[83] This was the first recognition of al Qaeda and its leadership to the American population. The two attacks clearly demonstrated al Qaeda's ability to practice improved operational reach. The operatives, tactics, and resources were provided by al Qaeda from a distant location to achieve success in Africa. Bin Laden's ability to move people, material, and money internationally and sustain them at the point of the tactical action were continuing to mature and contributed to al Qaeda's operational growth. The real growth is seen in

---

[80] Ibid., 115. See also Dan G. Cox, John Falconer, and Brian Stackhouse, *Terrorism, Instability, and Democracy* (Boston: Northeastern University Press, 2009), 193.

[81] Ibid.

[82] Ibid., 120.

[83] Ibid., 124.

the near simultaneous execution of two attacks in two different countries, al Qaeda's has significantly improved its operational reach.

As this learning organization attempted bolder operations, its demand for removal of American influence in the Middle East resonated with the United States Departments of State and Defense. Analyzing previous operations, an al Qaeda way of fighting began to emerge. Maintaining geographical distance from the operational core of al Qaeda proved to be a successful technique to ensure survivability of the organization. Similar to New York, the attacks on the United States embassies maximized al Qaeda's operational reach to pursue its strategic goals. Utilizing well trained combatants in an expeditionary fashion also added a layer of anonymity that insured operational reach would be successfully executed from Afghanistan. Al Qaeda had proved that conducting attacks on American targets could be achieved, yet lacked the ability to remove forces from the Middle East.

The repercussions of the attacks on the United States embassies placed al Qaeda in the crosshairs of United States military planners. Following the event, President Bill Clinton ordered Operation Infinite Reach, a series of cruise missile strikes on targets in Sudan and Afghanistan on August 20, 1998.[84] The mission proved ineffective and noncommittal which perpetuated al Qaeda's emboldened posture against the United States. The unwillingness of the US to commit manned fighter aircraft to make these strikes more successful also served to further develop bin Laden's impression that the US desire to avoid casualties was a center of gravity he could exploit.[85]

---

[84] Thomas G. Mahnken, *Technology and The American Way of War Since 1945* (New York: Columbia University Press, 2008), 207.

[85] Ibid.

Attack in Aden

The perceived lack of interest from the United States to engage in combat was reinforced by the event in the port of Aden. Veering from its successful employment of a truck bombs against buildings, al Qaeda's approach to attack USS Cole showed an organization willing to adjust its tactics in an attempt to achieve a different outcome.

On the morning of 12 October 2000, the USS Cole reached Aden harbor for a routine fuel stop. Around 11:18am local time, a small craft approached the port side of the destroyer, and an explosion occurred, putting a 40-by-40-foot gash in the ship's port side.[86] The blast hit the ship's galley, where the crew was lining up for lunch. The crew fought flooding in the engineering spaces and had the damage under control by evening, but throughout the day it was a close call and had things gone differently the ship could have sunk.[87]

In June 2001, an al Qaeda recruitment video featuring bin Laden boasted about the attack and encouraged similar attacks. Al Qaeda had previously attempted a similar but less publicized attack on the U.S. Navy destroyer the USS *The Sullivans* while in port at Aden, Yemen, on January 3, 2000, as a part of the 2000 millennium attack plots.[88] The plan was to load a boat full of explosives and explode near *The Sullivans*. However the boat al Qaeda employed was so overloaded with explosives that it sank, forcing the attack to be abandoned.[89] The adjustments to loading and rigging of explosives on the boat resulted in an extremely successful attack against the Cole. Once again, this demonstrates that al Qaeda was implementing the lessons learned from

---

[86] Department of Defense USS Cole Commission, *USS Cole Commission Report* (Washington, DC: GPO, 2001), 12.

[87] Ibid., 14.

[88] Bartholomew Elias, *Airport and Aviation Security: U.S. Policy and Strategy in the Age of Global Terrorism* (New York: Auerbach Publications 2009), 112.

[89] Ibid., 114.

tactical actions in its campaign into future actions to improve its performance as it constantly adjusted its lines of operation to support its main strategic goal.

Planning for the first failed attack was discussed at the Kuala Lumpur al Qaeda Summit shortly after the attempt, which was held from January 5 to January 8, 2000. Along with other plotters, it was attended by Khalid al-Mihdhar, who then traveled to San Diego where he established a close relationship with Anwar al-Awlaki.[90]

The results were a change in procedures gave al Qaeda an opportunity to gain international recognition and a chance to move a step closer to their goals through the successful attack against the USS *Cole*. The United States responded by looking internally at the problem and concluded that a refinement to rules of engagement for the Navy would be sufficient in combating these types of attacks. Ultimately, the al Qaeda organization was chastised by the international community for the attack but never received a direct military response. The United States also continued partnership with Middle Eastern countries and increased presence throughout the region. Al Qaeda's operational reach had proven to be a crucial aspect of their operations. It utilized this element to its furthest extent without degradation in its ability to execute attacks on two occasions in the same port. The organization's attacks also revealed the refined center of gravity analysis. Al Qaeda believed that by targeting government officials and military service members in the area would influence the American population to demand a removal troops from the Middle East region, much as had occurred after the bombing of the United States Marine Corps barracks in Beirut, Lebanon in 1983.[91] Although prior attempts had yet to achieve that goal, al Qaeda's process of increasing the cost in American lives to remain in the Middle East illustrates an organization that cognitively pieced together a sequence of attacks to pursue a strategic goal.

---

[90] *9-11 Report*, 343.

[91] Brian M. Jenkins, "The Organization Men," 14.

Attack in America

The final event of al Qaeda's American campaign fully developed in the fall of 2001. The horrific events that occurred early in the morning on September 11, 2001 showed a determined al Qaeda willing to attack civilian objectives to gain an effect on the center of gravity. The attack presented a new level of sophistication in tactics and planning, and al Qaeda's practice of operational art remained consistent with previous operations to pursue its strategic goals.

The attacks on September 11th were a series of four coordinated suicide attacks upon the United States in Washington, D.C. and New York. On that Tuesday morning, 19 terrorists from Al-Qaeda hijacked four passenger jets.[92] The hijackers intentionally crashed two planes into the Twin Towers of the World Trade Center in New York City; both towers collapsed within two hours. Hijackers crashed another flight into the Pentagon in Arlington, Virginia. The fourth jet crashed into a field near Shanksville, Pennsylvania after passengers attempted to retake control before it could reach the hijackers' intended target in Washington, D.C. Nearly 3,000 people died in the attacks.[93] Reports indicated hijackers stabbed and killed pilots, flight attendants, and one or more passengers in their initial effort to take control of the planes, and then claimed they had bombs on board to scare the passengers into passivity. In their final report, the 9/11 Commission found the hijackers had purchased multi-function hand tools and assorted knives and blades. The FBI found no traces of military or commercial explosives at the crash sites, proving the attackers had not brought explosives onto the flights.[94]

Two buildings in the World Trade Center Complex collapsed due to structural failure. The South Tower collapsed at 9:59 a.m. after burning for 56 minutes in a fire caused by the impact of United Airlines Flight 175. The North Tower collapsed at 10:28 a.m. after burning for

---

[92] *9-11 Report*, 19.

[93] Ibid., 238.

[94] Ibid., 22.

102 minutes.[95] Although the buildings had been designed to withstand fires for longer periods, it was later determined that the impact of the planes had blown the fireproofing off of the steel support members, leading to their failure. Although bin Laden, a trained engineer, had hoped the building would collapse above the points the planes struck at, he was almost as surprised as the New York City firefighters when the initial floors collapse led the buildings to pancake, completely destroying the structures.[96]

In a September 2002 interview, Khalid Sheikh Mohammed and Ramzi bin al-Shibh, who experts believe organized the attacks, said Flight 93's intended target was the United States Capitol Building, not the White House.[97] During the planning stage of the attacks, Mohamed Atta, the hijacker and pilot of Flight 11, thought the White House might be too tough a target and sought an assessment from Hani Hanjour, who would later hijack and pilot Flight 77. Mohammed also said al-Qaeda initially planned to target nuclear installations rather than the World Trade Center and the Pentagon, but decided against it, fearing things could get "out of control."[98] Final decisions on targeting, according to Mohammed, were left in the hands of the pilots.

The synchronized attacks on September 11th displayed to the world that al Qaeda was an organization that could not be ignored. Although most Americans, at this point in time, had never heard of al Qaeda, its sequential operations in recent years came to surface and a new belligerent emerged in world. The logical process of placing the attacks along a line of operation facilitates understanding of how al Qaeda pursued its objective to remove American forces from the Middle East. September 11th became the final operation along al Qaeda's lines of operation in the American Campaign. The series of attacks gradually elevated in destruction and casualties

---

[95] Ibid., 20.

[96] Bodansky, *Bin Laden*, 2-25.

[97] *9-11 Report*, 312.

[98] Ibid., 154.

attempting to raise the cost of al Qaeda's political objective beyond its value to the United States. The organization's analysis that the will of American people was the center of gravity appeared to be accurate. Al Qaeda's miscalculation of how to influence the center of gravity became evident in the final attack in the American campaign. Although they considered the impact of attacking the center of gravity inappropriately when they elected not to target nuclear facilities, for fear or the response it would provoke, they apparently were unable to understand that for the United States, massive civilian casualties would be as unacceptable as widespread nuclear contamination.

The American campaign revealed al Qaeda as an adaptive organization continually pursuing strategic objectives. The gaps in time showed a patient, thinking organization that only applied the strength of its operational reach when the opportunity appeared. The elements of operational art practiced in this case study revealed al Qaeda as a practitioner of operational art and an adaptive organization willing to learn from its experiences.

The European Campaign

Al Qaeda's attempt to divide the coalition of the willing during the war in Iraq materialized in the Madrid attacks on March 11, 2004 and the British bombings on July 7, 2005. The coordinated attacks focused on disrupting the public transit system and creating mass casualties throughout both cities. These events portrayed al Qaeda utilizing operational reach, along a line of operations, to attack a center of gravity. In the first case the results were exactly what al Qaeda expected, as a new political party in Spain was elected and rapidly ended Spain's participation in the war in Iraq, withdrawing the last of their troops on May 27, 2004.[99] The

---

[99] British Broadcasting Corporation, "Last Spanish Troops Leave," British Broadcasting Corporation, http://news.bbc.co.uk/2/hi/3734751.stm (accessed Apr 1, 2012).

second case in England, although successful in the tactical execution, revealed a misunderstanding of how the population (center of gravity) would react to terrorist attacks.

In a message directed at Europe, bin Laden threatened European nations to withdrawal forces from Afghanistan and stop all support for United States' operations in Iraq. He conveyed the message that United States forces would leave Iraq, leaving the responsibility on the European Forces to finish the war.[100] This threat loomed over all European forces contemplating whether to support the United States as questions of America's resolve to endure two protracted wars shaped the decisions of European leaders.

Attack in Spain

During the peak of Madrid rush hour on the morning of Thursday, March 11, 2004, ten explosions occurred aboard four commuter trains.[101] All the affected trains were traveling on the same line and in the same direction between Alcalá de Henares and the Atocha station in Madrid. It was later reported that thirteen improvised explosive devices had been placed on the trains. Bomb disposal teams arriving at the scenes of the explosions detonated two of the remaining three bombs in controlled detonations. Controversy regarding the handling and representation of the bombings by the government arose with Spain's two main political parties, Spanish Socialist Workers' Party and Partido Popular, accusing each other of concealing or distorting evidence for electoral reasons. The bombings occurred three days before the general elections in which incumbent José María Aznar's Partido Popular's was defeated, despite his small but narrowing lead in opinion polls.[102] Immediately after the bombing, the leaders of the Partido Popular claimed evidence indicating the Basque separatist organization Euskadi Ta Askatasuna (ETA)

---

[100] Osama bin Laden, "Leave Afghanistan," Cable News Network, http://edition.cnn.com/2007/WORLD/meast/11/29/bin.laden.message/index.html (accessed Apr 1, 2012).

[101] David Malone, *Bin Laden's Plan: The Project for the New Al Qaeda Century* (Bloomington: Trafford Publishing, 2005), 82.

[102] Ibid., 84.

was responsible for the bombings, an outcome generally thought favorable to the Partido Popular's chances of being re-elected. The claim was significant, because assigning Islamist responsibility would have had the opposite effect, as it would have been seen as a consequence of the Partido Popular government taking Spain into the Iraq War, a policy very unpopular with Spaniards.[103] Unfortunately for José María Aznar's this narrative was unsuccessful as it was untrue.

Immediate reactions to the attacks in Madrid were several press conferences held by the Spanish minister of interior of José María Aznar's government involving ETA. The Spanish government maintained this theory for two days. Because the bombings occurred only three days before the general elections in Spain, the situation had many political interpretations. The massacre also took place exactly two and a half years after the September 11th terrorist attack on the United States in 2001. Other interpretations of this date since emphasize the fact that the attack in Spain took place exactly 911 days after the bombings in New York and Washington, D.C. The United States also initially believed ETA was responsible, but then raised the possibility that Islamists were responsible.[104]

Statements issued shortly after the Madrid attacks from Lehendakari Juan José Ibarretxe, identified ETA as the prime suspect according to the government's theory. But the ETA, which usually claims responsibility for its actions, denied any wrongdoing.[105] Evidence later surfaced that strongly pointed to the involvement of extremist Islamist groups, from a Moroccan Islamic Combatant Group.[106]

---

[103] Ibid., 85.

[104] W. Timothy Coombs and Sherry J. Holladay, ed., *The Handbook of Crisis Communication* (Hoboken: Wiley-Blackwell Publishing, 2010), 451.

[105] Wayne Anderson, *The ETA: Spain's Basque Terrorists* (New York: Rosen Publishing Group, 2003), 26.

[106] Coombs and Holladay, *Handbook of Crisis*, 457.

Although ETA has a history of mounting bomb attacks in Madrid, the March 11 attacks far exceeded the scope of their previous attacks. This led some experts to point out that the tactics used were more typical of Islamist militant extremist groups, perhaps with links to al Qaeda, or maybe to a new generation of ETA activists using al Qaeda as a role model. Observers also noted that ETA customarily, but not always, issues warnings before its mass bombings and that there had been no warning for this attack. Europol director Jürgen Storbeck commented that the bombings "could have been ETA, but we're dealing with an attack that doesn't correspond to the modus operandi they have adopted up to now."[107]

Political analysts believed ETA's guilt would have strengthened the Partido Popular's chances of being re-elected, as this would have been regarded as the death throes of a terrorist organization reduced to desperate measures by the strong anti-terrorist policy of the Aznar administration. On the other hand, an Islamist attack would have been perceived as the direct result of Spain's involvement in Iraq, an unpopular war that had not been approved by the Spanish Parliament.[108]

On March 12, 2004, Spaniards took to the streets protesting against the bombings in a government-organized demonstration to condemn ETA, which at the time was being blamed for the attacks. Vigo, Spain, which has a population of 300,000 inhabitants, saw 400,000 demonstrators on its streets.[109] The protests were peaceful and included members of the leading political parties marching together down Madrid's Paseo de Castellana in solidarity against terrorism. More than two million people convened on Madrid's streets chanting: "Not everyone is

---

[107] Ewen MacAskill and Richard Norton-Taylor, "From Bali to Madrid, attackers seek to inflict ever-greater casualties" The Guardian, http://www.guardian.co.uk/world/2004/mar/12/alqaida.spain , (accessed Apr 1, 2012)

[108] Coombs and Holladay, *Handbook of Crisis*, 458.

[109] Ibid.

here, 191 are missing, we will never forget you." There were also people wondering, "Who did it?" in reference to the "lack of information provided by the government."[110]

The following day, Spanish authorities arrested three Moroccans and two Indians. At the scene the police found a number of clues, such as a cassette tape with verses of the Koran in a white Renault Kangoo van in Alcalá de Henares—that pointed to al Qaeda, or at least Islamic involvement.[111]Again the people of Madrid took to the streets, mainly congregating in the Puerta del Sol plaza, where there were a number of government buildings.[112] This time the mood was not peaceful. The crowd on Puerta del Sol chanted and bashed bottles and dustbin lids in a demonstration of anger towards Aznar. Meanwhile, people gathered in unofficial demonstrations in front of Party Partido offices in all the major cities in Spain.[113] More importantly, the slim lead that José María Aznar's Party had enjoyed at the polls evaporated.

The result of al Qaeda's actions revealed an accurate center of gravity analysis and was the first action in a line of operation aimed at getting the major European supporters of the United States to withdraw their forces from Iraq. The missteps from the government immediately following the attacks, and mass demonstrations swayed an entire population to elect a government that would withdrawal from combat in the Middle East. Al Qaeda's analysis of the internal turmoil of the state revealed a political party that was reliant on popular support. Spain's center of gravity was identified as the population and al Qaeda exploited the gaps between the people and the elected government. The coordinated attacks, the false reports of responsibility, and the ongoing war in Iraq exacerbated the cost of the political object beyond the value to Spain.

---

[110] Ibid., 459.

[111] Ibid., 461.

[112] Alison Pargeter, *The New Frontiers of Jihad: Radical Islam in Europe* (Philadelphia: University of Pennsylvania Press, 2008), 115-117.

[113] Ibid.

Al Qaeda's analysis of the center of gravity depicted an organization readily practicing operational art.

Al Qaeda's manifested its extended operational reach to employ tactics against the center of gravity in Spain to achieve a strategic goal for the organization. The process by which al Qaeda implemented operational reach transitioned to a new form with the Madrid bombings. The individuals that were responsible for the attacks, foreigners, were resourced and trained from outside of Spain. Al Qaeda's ability to exploit power at great distances and overcome the difficulties of the Spanish environment proved successful. Europe now had to adjust its tracking mechanisms to defeat this style of operations. The adjustments made in European security forced al Qaeda to reflectively look at new ways to achieve its goals and maintain its operational reach. A shift in the way operational reach was to be achieved, a change in means, came to fruition in the second operation of the European campaign.

Spain was the first in attack in the campaign to expel European forces from Iraq and Afghanistan. The success of the operation caught the world by surprise, but allowed al Qaeda to prepare the second operation of its campaign. Now that Spain had effectively severed its support of the Iraq war, a new operation in England could be attempted. This was an opportunity to dismantle the United States' coalition to combat al Qaeda in Iraq and Afghanistan by attacking its most important partner in the Global War on Terror.

Attack in England

In an attempt to reinforce success, al Qaeda initiated a spectacular synchronized attack on England's transportation system on July 7, 2005. In the second operation of the European campaign, indicators of operational art are evident when one compares this incident with the Madrid bombings. Al Qaeda attacked England's population, the center of gravity, by using homegrown terrorists cells funded from afar to bomb key transportation systems in the pursuit of achieving a break up of European support for United States operations in Iraq and Afghanistan.

36

On the morning of Thursday, July 7, 2005, four Islamist home-grown terrorists detonated four bombs, three in quick succession, aboard London underground trains across the city and later a fourth, on a double-decker bus in Tavistock Square.[114] Fifty-two people, as well as the four bombers, were killed in the attacks, and over 700 were injured. The explosions were caused by homemade organic peroxide-based devices packed into rucksacks. The bombings were followed exactly two weeks later by a second series of attempted attacks, but these were thwarted by alert citizenry and police.[115]

Protests and political upheaval did not result from the attacks in England. If al Qaeda's strategic goal was to force England to abandon its mission in Iraq, it simply did not work. However, as the war deteriorated and the threat to the homeland of England was felt, it would be false to assert that the bombings had no effect on the eventual unpopularity of the war.[116]

The center of gravity analysis conducted by al Qaeda prior to this campaign was successful in the Spanish operation, but unsuccessful in England. The center of gravity in both operations was deemed to be the population and political support for ongoing military operations. Al Qaeda's hoped to affect foreign policy through the domestic political process. Simply put, al Qaeda wanted to send the message that it was not worth the cost to side with the United States in its war against Iraq and Afghanistan.

Although there were only two major events on the western European homeland, these events can be viewed using the graphical depiction of lines of operations. The two attacks represent operations on those lines, with the goal of collapsing and splitting of the coalition. The attacks had a logical flow and the objectives were realistic. The attack in Spain was the most successful of any al Qaeda operation to date when viewed from a strategic level. The tactical

---

[114] Intelligence and Security Committee, *Report Into the London Terrorist Attacks on 7 July 2005* (London: The Licensing Division, 2006), 3.

[115] Ibid., 22.

[116] Ibid., 37.

actions in Spain caused a shift in the domestic political environment that resulted in the exact strategic goal the organization was seeking. Like any good commander, the al Qaeda leadership attempted to mimic success in England, however the public and the political establishment, similar to the United States, became more infuriated than intimidated. The attacks in Spain and England represented operations in a well defined sequence, synchronized in purpose to sever lines with the United States. The use of lines of operations while not completely successful in this campaign demonstrates al Qaeda's effective implementation of operational art.

Perhaps the most impressive element of operational art that characterizes al Qaeda operations throughout the world and particularly in this campaign was its operational reach. The ability to maintain global lines of communication and prevent culmination of its cells still baffles investigators and intelligence services. Al Qaeda operatives were radicalized and deployed to the locations of their attacks for from thousands of miles away. Additionally, special training and experts were planted into these countries to plan, prepare and execute these complex missions. Staffing, equipping, and directing these tactical actions were the most difficult tasks that the leadership had to accomplish at the operational level. It is one thing to conjure up plans to blow up busses and subways from caves in Afghanistan and Pakistan, but to orchestrate these operations from afar required a much greater level of detail and an understanding of the concept of operational reach.

The attacks in London demonstrated al Qaeda's shifting means of enabling operational reach. In reaction to the increased scrutiny on international travelers from the areas al Qaeda normally recruited from, the organization had increased its efforts to recruit disaffected Muslims from its targeted countries. This new method of enabling its operational reach by finding its forces within the legal population of the countries it targeted. This change allowed the organization to avoid many of the controls put in place to prevent its terrorist cells from traveling as they had to attack the US in 2001 and Spain in 2004.[117] Training and resourcing, especially financial, was still provided by al Qaeda, but its operatives were harder to identify and intercept using this new tactic. Al Qaeda's global operational reach is the element of operational art that separates this organization from other terrorist entities.

In al Qaeda's European campaign, its strategic objective was to split the coalition of the willing during the war in Iraq. Al Qaeda utilized bombings of specific transportations systems in Spain and England as its tactical actions. The attacks were sequenced in time and space along lines of operations to achieve the single purpose of influencing the center of gravity by using home grown operatives to extend al Qaeda's operational reach. The evidence in the European campaign depicts an adaptive organization regularly practicing operational art.

Conclusion

The research demonstrates that al Qaeda has been practicing operational art throughout its campaigns. The framework used in the case studies of center of gravity analysis, lines of operation, and operational reach were constant planning factors in both examples. It is worth mentioning that this analysis does not delineate between good and bad operational art. There are examples in al Qaeda operations of faulty analysis, especially in their efforts to achieve leverage over their identified centers of gravity in the US and Europe. However, the fact that the analysis was completed shows a level of operational planning that is not expected of a non-state actor. Of the three elements analyzed in this monograph the data indicates that the center of gravity analysis conducted by al Qaeda has been misplaced in its operations against the United States, but exact in the attack on Spain. This faulty center of gravity analysis in the case of England and the United States resulted in unintended consequences that caused undue risk to the organization. The

---

[117] Ayman al-Zawahiri, "Al-Qaeda," British Broadcasting Corporation, http://news.bbc.co.uk/2/hi/middle_east/3047903.stm (accessed Mar 23, 2012).

resources required to execute these operations were finite and the operations could only be executed once. Al Qaeda assumed that by attacking the population of both of these countries it could raise the cost of the political object beyond its value to the United States and England. This miscalculation cost al Qaeda key experienced leaders as drone attacks and special operations killed many of their leaders, a result that may led to the degradation of the organization.[118]

Additionally, operational reach was a constant element characterized by al Qaeda operations prior to September 2001. However, this element of operational reach was severely hindered after 2001 on operations in the United States, but prevailed in the European theater. Al Qaeda adjusted its operational reach by shifting the way it employed tactical actions. The employment of homegrown terrorism, as seen in England, demonstrated an organization drastically changing how it executed operations and a willingness to decentralize its actions to achieve its strategic objectives. A new way of looking at force employment allowed al Qaeda to operationalize disenfranchised Muslims within countries to maintain and extend its operational reach. The threat of that kind of imported strike has grown since the Al-Qaeda Organization in the Islamic Maghreb promised to extend its Algerian jihad to Europe. Bin Laden deputy Ayman al-Zawahiri has repeatedly threatened Europe — and France in particular — as enemies of jihadist forces. Meanwhile, French President Nicolas Sarkozy's friendlier relations with the U.S. and relatively pro-Israel positions have only increased extremists' ire. Since his taking office last May, officials say, radical websites have cited Sarkozy's support of Israel — and his own Jewish ancestry — in calling for terror strikes against France.[119]

---

[118] Telegraph Media Group, "Al Qaeda Number 3 Killed By Spy Plane," The Telegraph, http://www.telegraph.co.uk/news/worldnews/asia/pakistan/1504718/Al-Qaeda-number-three-killed-by-CIA-spy-plane-in-Pakistan.html (accessed Apr 1, 2012).

[119] Isabelle Tahar Miller, "Sarkozy, Israel and the Jews," The Jewish Voice, http://www.pjvoice.com/v33/33007sarkozy.aspx (accessed Apr 1, 2012).

Finally, the two campaigns demonstrate how al Qaeda synchronized operations along lines of operations to achieve its desired end state. Lines of operation were a hallmark of the patient approach that al Qaeda developed in its campaigns, but this element became disjointed after the 2001 attacks, as a lack of command and control coherence overtook the organization due to pressure from the United States. The advantages obtained in decentralizing the actions to gain operational reach became the downfall to lines of operation in the European campaign. This inability to continue a logical sequence of events characterized al Qaeda throughout 2001-2008, and became an even bigger problem after the aggressive drone campaign against senior leaders undertaken in the Obama administration.[120]

Recommendations

The terrorist attacks of September 11, 2001 awakened the United States that al Qaeda had declared war by attacking New York in 1993 and that America was facing a complex and adaptive enemy. The attacks were planned, the reconnaissance was conducted and al Qaeda achieved spectacular results. Military planners however, have struggled to place the planning cycle of the enemy in a coherent format, often times reverting to religion and culture in an attempt to explain events and predict future activities. This monograph asserts that policymakers and military planners can view the actions of al Qaeda forces through the lens of operational art. Recognizing that al Qaeda understands and pursues some of the same doctrinal underpinnings of strategy, campaign, and operations are useful. After reviewing the case studies in the framework provided here, the task of analyzing the actions of al Qaeda become clearer and more defined.

This monograph can be used by analysts to better predict al Qaeda's future actions by applying US Army doctrine on operational art, and the elements of center of gravity, operational

---

[120] Jake Tapper, "The Terrorist Notches on Obama's Belt," American Broadcasting Company, http://abcnews.go.com/blogs/politics/2011/09/the-terrorist-notches-on-obamas-belt/ (accessed Mar 23, 2012).

reach, and lines of operations. Planners at the operational and strategic levels can utilize these tools to see through the complexity of the enemy and their goals through a familiar and already understood framework.

Accepting the fact that al Qaeda practices operational art, further research is needed to determine if it will be able to sustain this capability following the loss key leaders, to include bin Laden. Will al Qaeda be able to explore and innovate in the realm of operational art? The death of senior leaders could result in a gap of organizational knowledge on linking tactical variables to achieve strategic effect. In his far reaching work, *Winning Insurgent Wars*, Dr. Geoff Demarest clearly identifies that in every insurgency there is the opportunity to shorten the struggle by successfully targeting the *mens rea* of the movement.[121] Although the speed Dr. Demarest encourages counterinsurgents to achieve has not occurred against al Qaeda, the cumulative effects of nineteen years of focused targeting of al Qaeda's leadership may have achieved the desired effect, destroying the coherence of the group and degrading its ability to practice operational art. The importance of knowing one's enemy has transcended time and remains crucial to the development of operational plans. If recent operations against al Qaeda have been successful there must be an inquiry on what specific actions taken by the United States disrupted there capability to prosecute war.

Al Qaeda has practiced operational art, and although its current capability to do so may be degraded, it will certainly seek to restore this capability in the future. Having identified this capability, those who oppose al Qaeda and similar terrorist groups would be wise to clearly identify if and how al Qaeda's operational art was successfully degraded, to take steps in identifying and then repeating this accomplishment against other illegitimate groups that attempt to practice operational art in pursuit of their political agendas. Identifying groups that seek an

---

[121] Geoff Demarest, *Winning Insurgent War: Back to Basics* (Fort Leavenworth: Book Express Publishing, 2011), 96.

operational capability early could lead to successful targeting early enough in the cycle to achieve

the quick victory that Dr. Demarest espouses.

BIBLIOGRAPHY

Published Works

Alexander, Yohan and Michael S. Swetnam. *Usama Bin Laden's Al-Qaida: Profile of a Terrorist Network*. NY: Transnational Publishers, Inc, 2001.

Anderson, Wayne. *The ETA: Spain's Basque Terrorists*. New York: Rosen Publishing Group, 2003.

Atwan, Abdel B. *The Secret History of Al Qaeda*. Berkeley: University of California Press, 2006.

Bergen, Peter L. The *Osama Bin Laden I Know: An Oral History of Al-Qaeda's Leader*. New York: Free Press, 2006.

Bevy, Lawrence J. ed. *Al-Qaeda: An Organization To Be Reckoned With*. New York: Novinka, 2004.

Brown, Vahid ed. *Cracks in the Foundation: Leadership Schisms in Al-Qaida 1989–2006*. West Point: Combating Terrorism Center Press, 2007.

Howard, Michael and Peter Paret. *Carl Von Clausewitz, On War*. Princeton: Princeton University Press, 1984.

Coombs, W. Timothy and Holladay, Sherry J. ed. *The Handbook of Crisis Communication*. Hoboken: Wiley-Blackwell Publishing, 2010.

Corbin, Jane. *Al Qaeda: In Search of the Terror Network that Threatens the World*. New York: Nation Books, 2002.

Cox, Dan G., Falconer, John and Stackhouse, Brian. *Terrorism, Instability, and Democracy*. Boston: Northeastern University Press, 2009.

Cozzens, Jeffery B. "Approaching Al-Qaeda's Warfare: Function, Culture, and Grand Strategy." in *Mapping Terrorism Research,* edited by Magnus Ranstorp, 121-132. New York: Routledge, 2007.

Demarest, Geoff. *Winning Insurgent War: Back to Basics*. Fort Leavenworth: Book Express Publishing, 2011.

Dijk, Teun Van and Kintsch, Walter. *Strategies of Discourse Comprehension*. Waltham, Massachusetts: Academic Press, 1983.

Dolman, Everett. *Pure Strategy: Power and Policy in the Space and Information Age*. New York: Routledge, 2005.

Doran, Michael Scott. "Somebody Else's Civil War." in *How Did This Happen? Terrorism and the New War*, edited by James F. Hoge, Jr., and Gideon Rose, 31-52. NY: Public Affairs, 2001.

Dower, John W. *Cultures of War: Pearl Harbor / Hiroshima / 9-11 / Iraq*. New York: W.W. Norton & Co., 2010.

Elias, Bartholomew. *Airport and Aviation Security: U.S. Policy and Strategy in the Age of Global Terrorism.* New York: Auerbach Publications 2009.

Esposito, Alice F, ed. *Al Qaeda: Background, Evolution and Assessment.* New York: Nova Science Publishers, 2010.

Forrest, James J. F. *Countering Terrorism and Insurgency in the 21st Century.* Westport: Greenwood Publishing Group, 2007.

Galula, David. *Counterinsurgency Warfare: Theory and Practice.* St. Petersburg: Hailer Publishing, 2005.

Gray, Colin S. War, *Peace and International Relations: An Introduction to Strategic History.* New York: Routledge, 2008.

Gunaratna, Rohan. *Inside Al Qaeda: Global Network of Terror.* New York: Berkley Books, 2003.

_____. "Who is Al Qaeda?" *Jane's Intelligence Review*, Vol. 13, no. 8, (August 2001), http://www.mwarrior.com/alqaeda.htm (accessed Jan 23, 2012).

Handel, Michael I. *Masters of War: Classical Strategic Thought.* London: Frank Cass, 2001.

Harrison, Richard W. *The Russian Way of War: Operational Art, 1904-1940.* Lawrence: University Press of Kansas, 2001.

Hashim, S. Ahmed. "The Strategy of Usama Bin Laden and Al Qaeda." in *Newport Papers*, edited by Andrew L. Ross, 14-28. Newport: Naval War College, 2002.

Hoffman, Bruce. "Osama's Learning Curve." *The National Journal.* Vol. 33, No. 45. Washington, DC: GPO, 2002.

Huntington, Samuel, P. *The Soldier and the State.* Cambridge, MA: Harvard University Press, 1959.

Isserson, Georgii Samoilovich. *The Evolution of Operational Art.* Trans. by Bruce W. Menning. Moscow: The State Military Publishing House of the USSR People's Defense, 1937.

Jamieson, Perry D. *Khobar Towers: Tragedy and Response.* Washington, DC: GPO, 2008

Jenkins, Brian M. "The Organization Men: Anatomy of a Terrorist Attack." in *How Did This Happen? Terrorism and the New War*, edited by. James F. Hoge, Jr. and Gideon Rose, 8-25, New York: Public Affairs, 2001.

Kelly, Justin and Mike Brennan. *Alien: How Operational Art Devoured Strategy.* Strategic Studies Institute Monographs. Carlisle Barracks, PA: U.S. Army War College, 2009.

Kipp, Jacob W. "The Origins of Soviet Operational Art 1917-1936" in *The Historical Perspectives of the Operational Art,* edited by Michael Detlef Krause and R. Cody Phillips, 67-82, Washington, DC: GPO, 2005.

Krause, Michael D. and R. Cody Phillips. *Historical Perspectives of the Operational Art.* Washington, DC: United States Army Center for Military History, 2007.

Levy, Bernard-Henri. *Who Killed Daniel Pearl?* New York: Melville House Publishing, 2003.

Lewis, Bernard. "License to Kill: Usama Bin Laden's Declaration of Jihad." *Foreign Affairs,* (November 1998), http://www.foreignaffairs.com/articles/54594/bernard-lewis/license-to-kill-usama-bin-ladins-declaration-of-jihad (accessed Mar 14, 2012).

Mahnken, Thomas G. *Technology and The American Way of War Since 1945.* New York: Columbia University Press, 2008.

Malone, David. *Bin Laden's Plan: The Project for the New Al Qaeda Century.* Bloomington: Trafford Publishing, 2005,

Matheny, Michael R. *Carrying the War to the Enemy: American Operational Art to 1945.* Norman: University of Oklahoma Press, 2011.

McKercher, B. J. C., and Michael A. Hennessy. *The Operational Art: Developments in the Theories of War.* Westport, Conn.: Praeger, 1996.

Miller, Judith. *God Has Ninety-Nine Names.* New York: Simon & Schuster, 1996.

Mintzberg, Henry. *The Rise and Fall of Strategic Planning.* New York: The Free Press, 1994.

National Commission on Terrorist Attacks upon the United States. *9-11 Commission Report.* Washington, DC: GPO, 2004

Naveh, Shimon. *In Pursuit of Military Excellence: The Evolution of Operational Theory.* London: Frank Cass, 1997.

Netanyahu, Benjamin, ed. *Terrorism: How the West Can Win.* New York: Farrar, Straus, &Giroux, 1986.

Newell, Clayton R. and Michael D. Krause. *On Operational Art.* Washington, DC: Army Center for Military History, 2005.

Pargeter, Alison. *The New Frontiers of Jihad: Radical Islam in Europe.* Philadelphia: University of Pennsylvania Press, 2008.

Phillips, Cody. *Historical Perspectives of the Operational Art.* Washington, DC: United States Army Center for Military History, 2007.

Pierce, Albert C. "War: Strategy vs. Ethics, Ethics and Strategy?" PhD diss., University California, Berkley, 2002.

Pillar, Paul R. *Terrorism and U.S. Foreign Policy.* Washington, DC: Brookings Institute Press, 2001.

Riedel, Bruce. *The Search For Al Qaeda.* Washington, DC: Brookings Institution Press, 2008.

Rollins, John. "Al Qaeda and Affiliates: Historical Perspective, Global Presence, and Implications for U.S. Policy." in *Al Qaeda: Background, Evolution, and Assessment,* edited by Alice F. Esposito, 44-68. New York: Nova Science Publishers, Inc., 2010.

Schneider, James R. *Theoretical Paper No. Four. Vulcan's Anvil: The American Civil War and the Foundation of Operational Art.* Fort Leavenworth: United States Army Command and General Staff College, 2004.

Swain, Richard M. "Filling the Void: The Operational Art and the U.S. Army." In *Operational Art: Developments in the Theory of War,* edited by B.J.C. McKercher and Michael Hennessy. Westport: Praeger, 1996.

Trofimov, Yaroslav *The Siege of Mecca.* New York: Doubleday, 2007.

Turabian, Kate L. *A Manual for Writers of Research Papers, Theses, and Dissertations.* 7th ed. Chicago: University of Chicago Press, 2007.

Van Creveld, Martin. *Command in War.* Cambridge: Harvard University Press, 1985.

Vego, Milan N. *Joint Operational Warfare: Theory and Practice.* Newport: United States Naval War College, 2007.

Zaeef, Abdul Salam. *My Life with the Taliban.* New York: C Hurst & Co., 2010.

Websites

British Broadcasting Corporation. "Last Spanish Troops Leave." British Broadcasting Corporation, http://news.bbc.co.uk/2/hi/3734751.stm (accessed Apr 1, 2012).

Cameron, David. "A Strong Britain in an Age of Uncertainty: The National Security Strategy 2010." http://www.official-documents.gov.uk/ (accessed Apr 1, 2012)

Laden, Osama bin., "Transcript of Bin Laden's October Interview." Cable News Network, http://articles.cnn.com/2002-02-05/world/binladen.transcript_1_incitement-fatwas-al-qaeda-organization?_s=PM:asiapcf (accessed Apr 01, 2012).

_____. "God knows it did not cross our minds to attack the towers." The Guardian, http://www.guardian.co.uk/world/2004/oct/30/alqaida.september11 (accessed Apr 1, 2012).

_____. "Terrorism Against America Deserves To Be Praised" The Outlook Group, http://www.outlookindia.com/article.aspx?214141 (accessed Jan 23, 2012).

_____. "Declaration of War Against the Americans Occupying the Land of the Two Holy Places." http://www.pbs.org/newshour/terrorism/international/fatwa_1996.html (accessed Apr 1, 2012).

_____. "The Al Qaeda Handbook." United States Department of Justice, http://www.justice.gov/ag/manualpart1_1.pdf (accessed Mar 14, 2012).

_____. "Leave Afghanistan." Cable News Network, http://edition.cnn.com/2007/WORLD/meast/11/29/bin.laden.message/index.html (accessed Apr 1, 2012).

MacAskill, Ewen and Taylor, Richard Norton. "From Bali to Madrid, attackers seek to inflict ever-greater casualties." The Guardian, http://www.guardian.co.uk/world/2004/mar/12/alqaida.spain (accessed Apr 1, 2012)

Miller, Isabelle Tahar. "Sarkozy, Israel and the Jews." The Jewish Voice. http://www.pjvoice.com/v33/33007sarkozy.aspx (accessed Apr 1, 2012).

National Infrastructure Protection Center. "Terrorist Interest in Water Supply and SCADA Systems, Information Bulletin 02-001." National Water System, http://www.mrws.org/Terror/Bulletin.html (accessed Mar 14, 2012).

Telegraph Media Group. "Al Qaeda Number 3 Killed By Spy Plane." The Telegraph, http://www.telegraph.co.uk/news/worldnews/asia/pakistan/1504718/Al-Qaeda-number-three-killed-by-CIA-spy-plane-in-Pakistan.html (accessed Apr 1, 2012).

Tapper, Jake. "The Terrorist Notches on Obama's Belt." American Broadcasting Company, http://abcnews.go.com/blogs/politics/2011/09/the-terrorist-notches-on-obamas-belt/ (accessed Mar 23, 2012).

Zawahiri, Ayman al. "Al-Qaeda." British Broadcasting Corporation, http://news.bbc.co.uk/2/hi/middle_east/3047903.stm (accessed Mar 23, 2012).

US DOD Doctrinal Sources

U.S. Department of the Army. *Army Doctrinal Publication 3-0 Unified Land Operations.* Washington, DC: Government Printing Office, 2011

_____, *FM 3-0 Operations.* Washington, DC: GPO, 2008

_____. *FM 6-22 Army Leadership.* Washington, DC: GPO, 2006

_____. *USS Commission Report* Washington, DC: GPO, 2001